Bridget —

Here's to Being

LAZY!

— Cynthia
Damon

Other Books by
Cynthia D'Amour, MBA

How to Turn Generation Me
Into Active Members of Your Association

How to Recruit Generation Me

Members Tell All!

Go Team Go!
Strategies for Leading Today's Teams to Victory

Networking: The Skill
the Schools Forgot to Teach

Are You ONE Relationship Away
From Making BIG Money?

The American Society of Association Executive's
The Component Relations Handbook
(Chapter contributor)

The Lazy Leader's Guide to Outrageous Results

Cynthia D'Amour, MBA
Leadership Strategist

ISBN 978-0-9654600-6-4

Cover design by David Zinn

Printed by Jump Start Books

Quantity Discounts

To order five or more copies of **The Lazy Leader's Guide
to Outrageous Results** for your volunteer leaders, staff,
colleagues, friends, leadership classes - or people you know
who really need help, call 734-994-0097.

Dedication

To James and Raindrop
for putting up with me
- and supporting me in my mission
to help Lazy Leaders
build strong chapters
as a way to change the world.

Acknowledgements

Before I could walk I was volunteering – or at least that's how the story goes. I come from a long line of volunteer leaders with all four grandparents and my parents always stepping up to volunteer and lead their organizations.

I was trained to be a leader my entire life – and hope I continue to do them proud teaching others many of the lessons I learned from them.

Thank you to all of the volunteer leaders I have worked with. From my high school friends to the thousands of leaders I speak to every year. I am honored to be part of your quest to move your mission forward - and have learned from you.

I am grateful to the leaders at the Chapter Leaders Playground who started giving me feedback before the Playground was launched - and continue to keep me in tune with reality still today.

I appreciate the association executives, volunteer leaders, clients and friends who took the time to join me in exploring ideas, to give me very specific feedback on my manuscript - and challenge me to write my best book yet.

Finally to my husband, James Carl D'Amour. James has served as sounding board, caretaker, pulse taker and more. His support is deeper than the ocean is wide. He creates the space which makes all of this possible. Life with me can be an adventure. Thanks being in my life James.

- Cynthia D'Amour

- What's Inside -

- Become a Master at Developing Others

- Become a Master at Honing
  Your Own Leadership Skills

It's Time to Face the Truth

What does it take to be a chapter leader who gets outrageous results?

- Lots of work.

- Blood, sweat and tears.

- Determination.

You know the "rules"...

- Give 110% and you'll get great results.

- You only get out what you put into it.

- You just need to work harder - go the extra mile.

You've heard the lies and clichés – and embraced them.

- If they are so right, why isn't your chapter overflowing with committed, energetic volunteers?

- Why aren't you achieving outrageous results as a leader?

It's time to let go...

- If you really want to be the leader who will take your chapter to new heights, it's time to let go of outdated leadership concepts that don't work.

- It's time to let go of competing for your chapter's Martyr of the Year award.

It's time to be a Lazy Leader!

Chapter One

Welcome to
The Lazy Leader's Guide
to Outrageous Results

Get ready for some straight-talking, how-to advice by someone who's been in your shoes.

We aren't going to talk theory.

We are going to get down and dirty to spell out exactly what will work.

- How not to have to do it all.

- How to stop being a volunteer repellent with your 110% leadership commitment.

This book may make you uncomfortable.

- If it does, I hope you keep reading.

- It means you need to hear what I'm saying.

I'm going to challenge the ways of the martyr leader – which have become engrained in too many chapters as the only way to lead.

A commitment to the martyr approach can kill your chapter.

- The false belief it's easier to do it myself.

- Others are shut out because it's not how we do things here.

Being a martyr leader is not totally your fault.

Hard work as the key to success has been touted for too long.

Martyrs are celebrated as a survival strategy.

- Most people don't want to do 110%.

- If martyrs don't do the work, who will?

- Fear seals the deal.

And some good news...

- The martyr way exists because people don't know there's any other way to get work done.

- But there is an alternative.

It's the Lazy Leader way.

In this book, you will learn how to:

- Get more work done with less personal effort.

- Create a team of excited volunteers.

- And move your chapter's mission forward with outrageous results.

You'll explore the three key elements of the being a Lazy Leader.

- Embracing the way of the Lazy Leader.

- Being the party.

- Maximizing your Personal Leadership Velocity.

You'll be supported in your transformation to becoming a Lazy Leader.

- We will walk you through the transformation process.

- Teach you basic skills used by Lazy Leaders.

- Answer frequently asked questions.

By the end of this book, you'll understand the power and heart behind the Lazy Leader approach.

You'll know specific steps you can take to stop doing it all – and as a result generate outrageous results in moving your chapter's mission forward.

You'll also know where to find additional resources to help you on your way.

As you become the Lazy Leader, you will create the chapter you've always dreamed of having.

I am honored to be on this voyage with you – and can't wait to hear your success stories too!

Cynthia

Cynthia D'Amour, MBA
damour@peoplepowerunlimited.com
Founder, Chapter Leaders Playground

Chapter Two

Embrace the Lazy Leader

Okay, so you've heard about the Lazy Leader approach and are interested in giving it a try.

What's the first thing you need to do?

Embrace the Lazy Leader.

If you want to make this approach work, success begins with you.

Are you willing to focus on moving the mission forward through a team effort – rather than doing all the work?

This is huge.

Your work as a leader will change.

You'll focus on:

- Developing people rather than doing the work.

- Inviting people to a fun and meaningful experience – rather than expecting them to do everything your way with no questions asked.

- Celebrating the work of others – rather than moan about all the work you've had to do yourself.

As you can see, your success will be about the work of others – not about you.

- When it's time for announcements at chapter meetings, you'll encourage your volunteers to take the stage so they can get exposure and practice their speaking skills.

- At board meetings, you'll brag about the efforts of your team and give kudos to specific volunteers who are opening doors and making things happen.

- When you work the room at chapter events, you'll share stories of your successful volunteers - and invite others to the party.

If you have never worked with a team of happy, committed volunteers – this will be new territory for you to explore and enjoy.

Welcome to the Lazy Leader approach!

New Actions You'll Take as a Lazy Leader

1. When someone asks you to do work, you'll give a great referral.

Most people ask you to take on work because they can trust you will get it done – not because you are the perfect fit for the work.

As a general rule, they just want to make sure the work gets done.

As a Lazy Leader, you will become a master at giving others the opportunity to shine in your chapter.

When you give a referral...

- You open the door for someone else to get their needs met through being involved in your chapter.

- Your reputation as a cool leader grows.

- You honor yourself and your chapter by focusing on moving the mission forward - rather than doing the work yourself.

(You'll learn specific steps for giving referrals in chapter six.)

2. You'll make decisions based on people volunteering – rather than what you can do at the time.

You will no longer be limited by how full your personal plate is.

As you build your team of volunteers, you'll be able to expand the reach of your project or area of responsibility - and create an even bigger impact.

3. You will let go of determining ALL the tiny details.

When you personally do all the work, the tiny-detail decisions matter.

When you work with a team, others will want to put their fingerprints on the results. This includes making some decisions about the little things.

In chapter four, you'll learn how to define the end picture – what success looks like. In that process, you and the team will identify the project "must-haves."

The rest can be open to interpretation of team members – which increases their sense of ownership and commitment to the team.

4. You will value and celebrate the achievements of your team and team members more than what you have personally done.

When you embrace the Lazy Leader, success is all about others and their accomplishments.

You become the choreographer of the dance – rather than the featured dancer.

- You lend your support to your team.

- You lobby on their behalf.

- You become a master teacher and coach.

- You love celebrating with others.

- You never take credit - and always pass thanks on to your team.

You appear a bigger and better leader than you've ever been before because of how you look out for your people.

Benefits of Embracing
The Lazy Leader Approach

1. You won't have to do all the work.

You may say, "But I like doing all the work."

You probably enjoy the pay-offs of doing all the work more than actually doing the work.

Embracing a team of volunteers to help you will still give you the pay-off of leading the successful team.

NOTE: If doing the hands-on work is what you really enjoy, then perhaps you need to move aside if you are a committee chair or officer in your chapter.

Doing volunteer work is an important job in its own right.

As a volunteer leader, your focus is securing the long-term future of your chapter - and moving your chapter's mission ahead.

This means being strategic and involving others to maximize your impact - both now and moving forward.

When you do all the work yourself in a leadership role, you put the future of your chapter at risk.

- Less people are emotionally connected to the chapter.

- Retention starts to drop.

- Only a handful of people are left doing anything.

It's a vicious circle.

By embracing the Lazy Leader approach, you commit to the success and bountiful future of your chapter – and you no longer have to do all the work!

2. You'll have more space to be strategic.

Allowing others to help out creates "free time" you can now use to be more strategic in achieving your goals.

No need to just redo the same old thing - year after year.

You'll have the ability (and diversity of minds thanks to your team), to take a good look at where you are going and to explore what can be.

3. You won't have to have all the answers all the time.

It can be draining to have to always know what's going to happen, how it will work and what to do next.

By embracing the Lazy Leader approach, you'll have a team to debate options, explore alternatives and find better ways.

4. You'll be giving the gift of involvement.

You already know what a difference being involved in your chapter has done for you.

Now you will help others find their way in your chapter and benefit from involvement – no matter how small their contribution.

You will be a life-changer by helping others make a meaningful impact through working with you!

5. Your leadership legacy grows as a Lazy Leader.

Your legacy is no longer just a great project.

Your legacy will now include:

- All the lives you've touched.

- The skills you helped develop.

- The amazing difference your team has made by working together.

Your legacy as a Lazy Leader can help the world live up to its potential.

Once you've embraced the Lazy Leader within you, it's time to become the party...

Chapter Three

Be the Party!

The second key element of the Lazy Leader approach centers on you being the party.

Being the party infuses energy into the experience of volunteering with you.

Potential volunteers have a ton of options for where they can spend their time. Part of their decision will be based on what it feels like to work with you.

- When volunteers leave your meetings or events, are they pumped up and a feeling good about the time they invested to help you out?

- Or are they drained, bored or frustrated? (Which means they probably won't come back for the next meeting.)

There is an abundance of people who want to be involved in something cool – which could be working with you!

Fun is at a premium – and can give you an advantage in the quest to acquire time from volunteers.

Your goal as the Lazy Leader is to create an experience where people say, "We had a blast – and got a lot of work done too!"

When you become the party, you also become the leader people want to work with.

Seven Tips for Creating a Fabulous Experience

When you are the party, your meetings are transformed into experiences worth attending. Here are seven tips to boost volunteer attendance.

1. Be inviting.

Make an effort to invite people to get involved, to check out your team, to join the party.

Your welcoming attitude sets the stage for attendance - and excitement about what you are doing.

2. Project excitement – not desperation.

No matter how many volunteers you currently have (or don't have) promote your meeting as the party it will be.

If you act desperate for people to help out you become volunteer repellent.

No one wants to work with a "loser" team!

If someone says, "I heard you were struggling."

Put on a smile and reply, "Not any more. We're having a blast - and doing some great work together. Would you like to check us out?"

Notice the invitation to join at the end of the comment.

Too often struggling leaders talk about how hard they are working, all the time it's taking – and chase volunteers away with the impression it's 110% volunteer effort or nothing.

As the Lazy Leader, you are willing to take help where you can get it - and welcome even those who only have a few hours to help your team.

3. Give great notice.

Make sure you get meeting dates and agendas out in advance.

You want to give your volunteers time to invite their friends to your meetings.

Include meeting time and place on the agenda so new people know where to go. A cell number is an extra nice touch in case volunteers get lost or are running late.

4. Identify hot topics in advance.

Strategic conversations are part of what will make your meetings more fun.

Spending the bulk of face-to-face time listening to individuals give updates is an old school approach to meetings.

With today's technology, it's easy to take care of those reports in advance.

The opportunity to analyze, brainstorm and problem solve is what makes meetings more interesting for today's volunteers.

Identify upcoming strategic discussions on your agendas.

Encourage your team to start thinking about the issues in advance – and give them time to work their networks to explore potential solutions.

5. Create solutions at your meetings.

Don't arrive with all the answers already decided.

A big mistake people new to this approach make is showing up with their mind made up - and just going through the motions of allowing team members to participate.

There's nothing worse than participating in an exciting conversation to explore options and then having the chair say, "We've heard some new ideas – but I think we should just keep doing everything the way we've always done it."

- With this type of comment, you violate the trust your team members gave you by showing up for your meeting.

- They expected a valuable use of their time.

- Instead you just wasted it – with answers predetermined there is little reason for them to show.

**Being the party means volunteers get to participate
whenever they show up – a party is not about watching
one person have all the fun.**

6. Stimulate senses at your parties.

Activating senses increases the feeling of the experience –
rather than a boring meeting.

- **What do members hear when they walk in?**

  A warm welcome is important. Greet them
  by name. Music in the background can set the mood
  if available.

- **What do members smell in the air?**

  Is there fresh coffee? Something just baked?
  Fresh flowers? Candles?

- **What do members taste when the walk in?**

  Food is a big volunteer attractor – even if it's
  just candy on the table.

  (Bonus points for chocolate!)

  Overheard by team members walking out of a
  meeting, "Can you believe they didn't even serve us
  water or throw a few candies on the table. Doesn't
  feel like they care if we came or not."

- **What do members see when they walk in?**

  Does it look like you expected them? Is the meeting set up? Are there any fun touches – like decorative napkins or center pieces?

The more senses you purposely activate at your meetings, the less they feel like meetings – and more like experiences!

7. Consider using themes with your parties.

Tapping into a theme can be a way to add excitement to your team – especially as a project kick-off or to recharge the group's energy.

Here's a fun example...

A chapter's major fundraiser involved selling and installing green roping and wreaths for the Christmas season at local businesses.

This single fundraiser basically financed the chapter for the entire year – in a very nice way!

Planning always started in the summer.

One year, a creative chair hosted a Christmas in July party to kick off the project.

- There was the pre-meeting Christmas cookie baking party – which was also well attended.

- Meeting announcements were designed as holiday party invitations.

- The chair pulled out some Christmas decorations – including a life-size snowman proudly displayed on her front lawn.

- When members drove up to her house, they were greeted by Elvis singing holiday songs.

People were smiling and laughing before they made it in her house. The tone was set for the entire evening.

- The party was very well attended.

- They had a great meeting with terrific conversation.

- Members left excited to be on the team.

To keep her volunteers engaged, through the six months of work, the chair periodically found a way to pump up the meeting fun.

On a side note: A brand new member, who just came for the kick-off party, had an idea and connection which ended up increasing their revenues by 30%.

Adding a themed-element to your meetings can take some creative effort – and pay off like crazy.

(As a Lazy Leader, you might invite others to create meeting themes. It's not something you have to do by yourself.)

Common Resistance
to Being the Party

Okay, I already know what some of you are saying
about being the party.

Here are the most common things I hear about why
this approach won't work.

1. I'm not a funny person.

No one said you have to be funny. Being the party is about
the positive energy you project about your team and
their experience. Anyone can do it.

No jokes required to create a success.

**2. I don't have time to mess with all the extra work
to make meetings more fun.**

Who said you have to do the work?

There are people who would love to help you out with this –
if they know about the opportunity and feel appreciated.

Some teams hold internal mini-competitions to determine
who hosts the most fun meetings.

Plus, fun for many folks means simply being allowed to have
a voice and be involved.

3. We are a professional group – not a fun group!

Is it working for you to be totally serious and boring?

If yes, then great. You are good to go. Forget the party.

Usually the leaders who resist allowing some fun into their work the most are the same leaders who are struggling to recruit new members and volunteers.

There are many ways to have fun.

Adding fun can be as simple as starting your meeting with every member sharing their claim to fame since you last saw them. (Takes less than a minute/person.)

- Their claim might be something professional or personal.

- It's a positive accomplishment.

- Everyone gets their voice on the table and sets a positive tone for the meeting.

If you do this, you'll also find people lingering after the meeting to hear the rest of the story.

Your team will be more bonded - and your meetings more interesting.

4. This sounds like a waste of time to me.

Hmmm… since when is creating experiences making more volunteers excited about helping you out a waste of time?

It will take less time to be the party than doing everything by yourself.

5. Volunteering is the right thing to do – I shouldn't have to sell anything.

The challenge is there are hundreds of wonderful and worthy opportunities for people to volunteer their time.

Being the party is designed to make volunteering for your chapter or cause more attractive than the rest.

Consider Sandra's story...

Sandra had been a leader for more than ten years.

Her chapter was struggling and had a hard time attracting new members.

It was time for the annual recruitment attempt.

Sandra was talking to a young professional named Misty about all the volunteer opportunities in the chapter.

Misty listened respectfully and asked, "Sandra can you tell me what's in it for me to get involved?"

Sandra could not believe what she was hearing. Didn't Misty listen to anything she had just said?

"What do you mean?" Sandra demanded.

Misty replied earnestly, "I'm sort of interested in the chapter's big project. I need some help figuring out what's in it for me."

Sandra could feel the anger boiling in her blood again!

- She was so tired of younger members asking her what they could get by volunteering.

- Would she have done it for so many years if it was a waste of time?

- Plus it was the right thing to do!

Sandra clenched her teeth and was about to reply when Misty interrupted her, "Are you mad at me for some reason? You look like my mom when she's about to yell at me."

Sandra was shocked into silence.

Misty continued, "I'm new in my position at work. I love what your chapter is doing. I want to be involved. I need to be able to sell it to my boss. I thought with your experience you could help me spell the benefits out."

Looking down, Misty concluded, "I didn't mean to make you mad. I just needed help. It's okay if it's too much effort…"

Sandra felt horrible.

She usually considered herself a nice woman.

**Misty was asking her for help and she had taken it
as an insult.**

How many other young professionals had she scared away
by refusing to help them understand what was in it for them
to be involved?

The issue for most who volunteer is not whether they will
volunteer – it's where does it feel good to spend their time
in addition to the impact they'll be making?

6. My members don't like to have fun.

How do you know? Are you talking about those who are
currently active? Or those who you rarely see?

**If your meetings consist of simply giving reports and
being micromanaged by you – the lack of fun and
opportunity to be involved may be your biggest
volunteer repellant.**

Today's volunteers are looking for well-run experiences
where they have an opportunity to make a meaningful
impact. Being the party amplifies the experience for them.

7. I'm a VIP/CEO – not a clown! This is insulting!

Even your colleagues like to have fun. As an executive you
work long and hard hours.

Creating a welcoming and supportive community of peers
makes being at the top less lonely. Producing a meaningful
impact feels good too.

There are many ways to define being the party and having fun. The goal is to create the experience that generates happy, active and committed members.

8. Being the party sounds uncomfortable to me.

Being welcoming, involving and creative may require you to use some new skills – which may feel a bit uncomfortable at first. That's because the skills are new to you and you are very aware of what you are doing.

With practice, inviting people to join the party will be natural. Have faith and keep making those invitations!

Nine Ways to Speed the Growth of Your Party

Hopefully by now, you believe you can be the party – and it will pay off in more volunteers eager to help you move your mission forward.

To help you amp up your party making efforts, here are nine ways you can speed your growth and become a major volunteer magnet.

1. Tap the power of diversity.

Great parties have interesting people and discussions. People with different backgrounds will add richness to the experience of working with you.

Be the Party!

2. Recruit the recruiters.

There are some people who are natural inviters. When you welcome the recruiters on your team they are likely to bring others with them.

3. Celebrate early and often.

Don't wait to the end of your project or year to celebrate all your team achieves. Celebrate milestones achieved, doors that are opened – even personal team member accomplishments.

Celebration is a way for you to recognize the efforts of your team and reinforces the impact and progress you are making together!

4. Be a proud leader.

Let others know what's going on with your team. Advocate for individual team members. Share the exciting news about what you are accomplishing together.

As you do, you'll find more people want to be part of your action.

5. Be bodacious.

In your conversations and goals. Let's be real...

Growing by 10% is a yawner...

It's much more exciting to challenge team members to stretch how they currently do things.

It also helps unleash creativity – which many volunteers don't get to use very often.

<u>Extra benefit</u>: Strategic conversations about what needs to happen to achieve bodacious goals often give insights overlooked by smaller thinking.

Here's Megan's bodacious story...

For years the chapter set a goal of 10% membership growth.

They rarely achieved it.

They used the same recruitment plan every year – and just added new dates.

Megan agreed to be membership chair and was frustrated at the lack responses she got when asking for help with recruiting new members.

She decided to be bodacious and hold a party to brainstorm how to double membership that year.

- Many thought she was nuts.

- A few thought it might be fun to play with the idea and decided to attend.

At the brainstorming party, Megan challenged them to stretch their minds about what already existed.

She asked them three main questions:

- If we already doubled up our membership, what would it look like?

- What could we be able to differently thanks to all the new members?

- What would we need to differently to support so many new members?

At first, people struggled with the questions.

They had problems imagining so many new people.

Megan held firm with her questions.

She pulled answers from people by asking, "If we did have that many new members, what would your answer be?"

As momentum in answering Megan's questions picked up, the enthusiasm in the room grew.

- "Wouldn't that be cool?"

- "Wow! I never thought we could do that!"

Working through the "what would need to be different" question, they discovered a few things they could start to implement right away – like creating a better process to help guests and new members build connections with current members.

Megan's "crazy approach" transformed boring old
membership stuff into a new source of excitement
in the chapter.

**Did the chapter double up their membership by the end
of the year?**

- Not quite – but they did grow their chapter by 30%
  - instead of the normal 5%.

- Plus, with more members involved in making
  others feel welcomed, retention was the strongest
  it had been in years.

The bodacious approach paid off for Megan's chapter!

6. Welcome new ways.

People are not looking for the opportunity to do things
the way it's always been done.

**The same project run the same way year after year
becomes mindless work – not a party.**

When you invite new people to join the fun – no matter what
level they can commit at – you open the door to new ideas.

**Shut down all the new ideas and you'll lose
the new volunteers too.**

There may be times when it just hurts to hear new ideas
coming from people who haven't spent a fraction of the time
you have dedicated to your chapter or project.

Don't take their comments personally.

When they offer up suggestions, they are speaking simply from their point of reference.

They may have no idea you were the person who originally created the project - and the aspect they want to change was your crowning glory a few years ago.

They probably don't know - or may not remember.

It isn't personal.

You did a good job helping them get caught up in the passion of making the project the best it can be - and simply want to put their thumbprint on the success too.

When it hurts, breathe through it - rather than shoot down their ideas in anger.

Remember the ultimate goal of your project - and your personal goal to be a Lazy Leader who moves your mission forward by getting others involved.

Just like you did, they too need to feel like they own a piece of the project.

Tap into your questioning skills and help pull from them the answers to your concerns about change.

Your team may adopt the suggested changes, just part of them or perhaps none of them. It all depends upon identifying the best fit for your goals this year.

Participating in a strategic conversation where options are analyzed rationally can be very exciting.

When you welcome new ideas and celebrate a creative team, word will spread. More people will want to join your party – which is perfect for the Lazy Leader.

7. Use attractive language.

Host a party - not a committee meeting. Have interesting conversations - not just boring report outs.

Celebrate new ideas - not do things "Because I said so."

The words you use to describe working with you can attract or repel potential volunteers.

8. Enjoy having more fun.

Fun is a value these days – not an option.

If you are committed to being a Lazy Leader, it's going to be a way of life for you.

Might as well lean into it and enjoy it!

9. Hone your skills.

Martyr leaders often talk about giving 110% to their cause. As a Lazy Leader you want to welcome anyone willing to help move your mission forward.

Volunteers able give only 10 - 25% of their time and effort can still be valuable contributors to your team.

Think about it…

- A ten-minute phone call with the right person may open important doors.

- A team of volunteers who can give only two hours at a critical time may be the difference between success and failure.

- Guidance via email from an expert source can save your team hours of work.

Whether 10, 20 or even 45% volunteers, they still need to be invited to play, involved as part of the team - and appreciated.

Being a Lazy Leader able to work with more fluid teams requires you to develop some new skills.

Accelerate your growth by focusing on skills such as:

- Working with diverse teams.

- Running amazing meetings.

- Thinking like a marketer.

- Communicating with style.

- Developing future leaders through their work with you.

The Chapter Leaders Playground is a great resource
of how-to information about the skills you need to success
as a Lazy Leader. (www.chapterleadersplayground.org)

You can choose from more than 40 webinars each year
which are fun, interactive - and designed to take your skills
to a new level in an hour or less.

**You've committed to being a Lazy Leader and being
the party.**

**It's time to talk about your Personal Leadership Velocity -
and how maximizing it can help you achieve
outrageous results!**

Chapter Four

Maximize Your Personal Leadership Velocity

Your job as a chapter leader is to move the mission of your chapter forward.

You may serve on the board, lead the membership effort, chair the fundraising project, oversee professional development effort, etc.

As a Lazy Leader, you focus on moving your mission forward through the involvement of others – so you don't have to be a 110% volunteer any more.

The third key element in the Lazy Leader approach is maximizing your Personal Leadership Velocity.

- You want to move your mission forward as far as possible with as little personal effort as possible.

- You focus on finding the most efficient and effective use of your time.

The more you maximize your personal leadership velocity, the bigger impact you make with the least amount of personal effort.

What does this mean?

As a martyr leader, you will do all the work yourself. You may get the project done but no one else is involved.

As a Lazy Leader, you don't want your time soaked up by doing all of the work. You want to be able to work at say a 50% level - and still make sure the project gets done.

Getting more members involved on your team is one way to help you achieve your goal of completing the project with only a 50% commitment level.

Your Personal Leadership Velocity is now twice that of the martyr leader because you got the same work done with half the personal effort.

Huh?

In other words, when you maximize your personal leadership velocity, you get more work done with less effort.

You will focus on finding ways to make the best use of your time to move the mission forward.

At the end of this chapter, you can watch me crunch some numbers to see the actual impact of effort on your personal leadership velocity.

If numbers aren't your thing, don't worry.

As long as you understand maximizing your personal leadership velocity means getting more work done with less personal effort you are fine.

There are a variety of ways to increase your velocity.

Simply being more aware of what you are doing can have an impact. So can how you work with your team and individual volunteers.

Five Questions to Regularly Ask Yourself

Here are five questions you'll want to ask yourself – especially as you embrace the Lazy Leader approach.

1. Am I micro-managing?

Are you calling your volunteers every day? Are you calling vendors in advance to "help" the your volunteer succeed - and then calling the vendor after their interaction to correct any mistakes?

Are you breathing down your volunteers' necks too much? Are your volunteers tired of being corrected all the time – even before they take action?

Being a Lazy Leader means being okay with letting go of some of the details.

Work may not be exactly as you would do it - and who cares as long as it fits the agreed upon parameters?

When you micro-manage your volunteers you can soak up time by getting in their way. You may even chase them away - and have to do it all yourself.

Whether micro-managing or reclaiming the work, both actions slow up your personal leadership velocity. It now takes a lot more time from you to get the same work done.

2. Do I really need to have the final say in this?

If yes, why?

- Are you taking on the responsibility out of habit?

- Could you teach one of your volunteer the criteria for evaluating a job well done?

- Does it really matter what color the program is printed on – as long as they stay within budget and get the job totally done?

There are times when you need to have the final say. Probably more when you don't.

Giving volunteers some decision making ability helps increase their sense of ownership, feeling of impact – and commitment to volunteer for you. It also helps maximize your Personal Leadership Velocity.

3. Is this still relevant?

What are you doing that is no longer relevant to moving your mission forward?

Are there things you are doing because you've always done them – even if they are no longer the most efficient way?

If you were challenged to eliminate 10% of the work you and your team are doing, what would be the first to go? Why are you still doing it?

For example:

Allie's chapter traditionally held an annual recruitment dinner. It was quite the labor-intensive event – and held every year since the chapter was formed.

New to the committee, Allie asked how many people joined as a result of the dinner.

Older members gasped! "Why does it matter? This event is our tradition!"

Allie challenged, "Maybe so, but this event uses almost a quarter of our annual chapter budget. I just wonder if it's the best use of funds for moving our mission forward."

Steve, the committee chair, flipped his project book to the results section, "Well, last year we got one member, the year before two…"

Allie offered, "Maybe there are other ways to recruit new members. A year round approach creates more opportunities to join.

Plus if we make recruiting a normal part of our chapter experience we'll be able to free up lots of money to use elsewhere."

The idea was radical for the chapter – and yet made some sense too.

41

Allie was right.

The freed up money and volunteer time allowed the chapter to create a fabulous year – fueled by a new project and major membership growth.

Steve and others had never thought to ask why the chapter invested so much in an event which produced so little.
After all, it was tradition.

It's always good to take a periodic review of what you are doing to make sure you still need to do it.

Letting go of no longer useful steps frees up your time.
You are able to get the same project done with less effort – thus increasing your Personal Leadership Velocity.

4. Can someone else do this step?

Before you make effort to get work done, analyze what could be done by others.

It may be tempting to convince yourself, "It's easier if I do it myself" - but that's a short term strategy.

Investing in training someone may take some time up front - but will pay off over the months and years ahead.

Encourage your team to cross train members on their responsibilities so when they need someone to help out, it doesn't have to be you.

The more ways you can involve others in doing various steps in your project, the more time you free up for you – which increases your velocity.

5. Does this work energize me?

If you are doing work you don't enjoy, odds are good it will take you longer to do than something that's a great fit for your natural talents.

As a result, the time needed to get the work done is dramatically increased to accommodate your avoidance activities.

In most of these situations, you are better off referring the work to someone else – rather than saying "yes" in the first place. This is true even if you need to recruit a new team member to help out with the task.

Taking on work that's not a good fit for you and is an energy drainer - and slows your velocity.

Five Keys to Maximize Your Velocity Through Your Work with Teams

1. Start with the end in mind.

Before launching team members into action, create a picture together of what success will look like when the team's work is done.

- What will you see?

- What will happen?

- What will you hear people say?

- What kind of results will you achieve?

- Who will be involved?

- Can you create a paragraph or two describing the goal achieved?

The goal is not for you, as a Lazy Leader, to walk in with all the answers.

Instead, invite your volunteers to get involved in describing what success looks like.

By the end of the conversation everyone on the team should be excited about the answers to these defining questions.

Too often, martyr leaders walk in with the picture clear in their minds - down to the last detail.

The final big picture is a buzz of excitement in the martyr's mind – and not really necessary to share with others.

After all this is their year to be in charge.

The volunteers are simply lackeys who are there to do whatever they ask, exactly as told - and be okay with massive micro-managing.

Most times, to the secret relief of the martyr leader, the volunteers go away.

With no volunteers left, the martyr leader has 100% control to do things exactly as they like. In addition, they get extra attention by moaning about how no one is willing to help.

The martyr leader has totally slowed down their velocity and is not worried about moving the mission forward – just doing their project their way.

A different approach…

The Lazy Leader has no interest in doing all the work nor having all the answers as far as the big picture goes.

Sure there will be some parameters like budget or focus which may be predetermined. Involve your members in defining the rest.

The more they buy-in to the possibility you are creating, the more they are going to take ownership and stick around to the do the work.

By involving others in the big picture creation you increase your velocity.

2. Communicate progress regularly with all.

As a Lazy Leader, you want everyone involved in the success of the project – even if they can only give 10-20%.

One way to do this is to regularly share where the project stands, what needs to happen, who has completed the work and found success.

- Build in mini-milestones so every meeting involved celebrating progress.

- Use tools such as Excel and online space to make status updates easy to do.

Fuel the pride and sense of accomplishment of your volunteers. Help them realize all they have done together.

Regular status updates also keep you on top of what needs to be done – but not so you can do it. Instead you can find help, give support or cheer on other volunteers who need it.

These updates help make sure you and the team bring everything in on time - and well done.

Using a Lazy Leader approach does not mean a decrease in quality output – only that you are able to get more done with less personal effort.

3. Resist encouraging martyrdom in your team members.

There will always be a few folks who are willing to say "yes" to anything you ask and will work their fingers to a bone.

Resist the temptation to dump everything on them. Sure it's an easy way to make less work for you – but you also increase the risk involved in your project.

What happens if that person gets sick, transferred or hit by the beer truck? Will you know what they were working on? What still needs to be done? Will you have trained people in the wings ready to step up?

It's much easier and less risky to encourage your team to be the party and include others in their work. Challenge your team with questions such as:

- Are there others we should involve?

- Are there skills we need to learn?

- Could some one-time helpers ease our load?

Remember more involvement means more people committed to moving the chapter's mission forward – and increases your personal velocity too!

4. Coach your team members to tap into resources beyond the actual team.

Just because they are on the team, does not mean they have to have all the answers.

A lot of time can be wasted, when members try to do everything internally. Involving other chapter members can provide the resources needed to get to the next level.

Consider this...

A committee suffered for a year trying to raise funds for a benefit project. No matter how hard the six members made outbound calls, created beautiful flyers or lovely mailers, nothing seemed to work.

They needed to raise $50,000 and after a year had less than $2,000.

There were over 300 people in their chapter – but they never asked other members for help. After all, this was the committee's job.

With a little coaching from me, at the next chapter meeting, the team did an informative presentation about how cool the project would be - and asked if any members had ideas about how to raise the money.

- A handful of members present had ideas - and few even made inquiries on behalf of the committee to employers.

- Within ten days, the committee had more than $25,000 dollars committed to the project.

- By the end of the year, the project was totally funded.

Without reaching out to others, it is questionable if the project would have survived.

Ignoring your potential resources can have quite the negative impact on velocity!

5. Focus on team achievement.

During your meetings, appreciate the contributions individuals made. And in the meeting wrap up, focus on team achievement – how far you have come and where you are going next.

The reason behind this?

With a team focus, rather than a superstar focus, everyone's contributions matter.

Your 10-20% volunteers need to feel like they made a meaningful impact - as well as those giving more.

A simple call may open doors endless hours of hard work would never break through.

The more you build the spirit of the team, the more likely folks are to stick around.

With a celebration of team achievement, it will become too much fun attending your meetings to dream of missing one.

Four Ways to Maximize Your Velocity by Working with Team Members

You can also impact your velocity as you work with individual members. Here are four examples.

1. Focus on building relationships.

Relationships are built across time and fuel trust.

The better you know your members, the less it is about work and more about them having a positive, relative experience.

49

When your volunteers feel like you care about them, they are more likely to complete their work.

Help your volunteers get to know each other as well. Friendship can be powerful glue in keeping members involved.

2. Mind your manners with your volunteers.

Treat them with respect. Appreciate their efforts to help you. Write fabulous thank you notes.

When is the last time you got a thank you note which made you smile inside and out?

That's the kind of appreciation you want to give your members.

Don't just say thanks...

- Tell them what they did and why it mattered.

- Show you understand the effort they made.

- Give them feedback you got from others about their contribution.

Cards sent via snail mail are extra special. They show you cared enough to take the time to send the card. They also look great on a bookcase so others can see too.

(Keep a box of greeting cards ready to go in your desk to make this easier to do.)

If you have no time for cards, at least send a personalized email – rather than nothing.

Whether greeting card or email, a descriptive thanks has the potential to change lives – and helps keep members committed to your team.

3. Help your team members achieve their personal goals.

Everyone has a personal reason or goal in mind when they say "yes" to volunteer with you.

As a Lazy Leader, you want to know what each member's goals is – and help all of them get their needs met by volunteering with you.

Get into the specifics of what they are looking for.

- If they want to learn how to manage a team better by working with you, make them your assistant.

- If they want to make a difference, find out what kind and regularly help them see the connection between their efforts and their goals.

- If they want to meet cool people, find out who they are talking about - and help make introductions.

The more the word gets out about your commitment to helping members achieve their personal goals, the more likely others will want to volunteer for you as well.

4. Become a master coach.

Learn to pull information from your volunteers instead
of always giving them the answers.

- Teach them to problem solve and to find confidence
  in their conclusions. (Discussed more in chapter six.)

- Show them you trust them to have good sense
  and come up with a correct solution.

**Volunteers are often diminished to mindless worker bees
by martyr leaders who want to keep all the control.**

As a Lazy Leader, your goal is to develop your volunteers
so they are prepared to make the right decisions for moving
your project forward.

**As their skills grow, they can turn into leaders on
your team and help develop the next layer of volunteers.**

There are many ways you can work with individuals to
help them be stronger on your team – and thus increase
your Personal Leadership Velocity.

Maximizing
Personal Leadership Velocity
by the Numbers

For those of you who like to see numbers in action,
I've prepared some samples to show you how you can
impact your Personal Leadership Velocity.

Let's start in the beginning...

Velocity = output/input

In other words, personal leadership velocity describes how fast you are moving your mission forward based on your efforts.

Typically personal leadership success is based on how hard a person works.

Value is placed in buckets of personal sweat instead of impact on moving the mission forward.

Too often, the leader who works the hardest, moans the loudest, does it all themselves has their martyr status rewarded by being named martyr, er, member of the year.

The Lazy Leader approach is committed to moving the mission of the chapter forward rather than acquiring personal accolades for scaring off volunteers, doing things the way they've always done it - and jeopardizing the future of the chapter by not welcoming new team members.

The Lazy Leader is committed to finding ways to make every moment count as much as possible.

Applying the personal leadership velocity concept...

Case #1: The martyr leader gives 100% and gets one project done – with little help from anyone else.

Martyr Velocity = output/input = 100% successful project/100% personal capacity = 1.0 projects/effort

Case #2: The Lazy Leader, thanks to being the party and allowing others to do the work, is only working at a 50% level not breaking any major sweat - and still gets one successful project done.

Lazy Leader Velocity = 100% project/50% personal capacity = 2.0 projects/effort

Case #3: Because the Lazy Leader encouraged volunteers at all levels of effort to be part of the party, a one-time attendee made a referral which made project success soar with a 20% increase – and no major increase in work!

Lazy Leader Velocity = 120% project/50% personal capacity = 2.4 projects/effort

Case #4: The martyr leader also wants to grow the project to 120%. He had no help, so he rearranges his life to eke out 110% for the duration of the project.

Martyr Velocity = 120% project/110% personal capacity = 1.09 projects/effort

Not a very impressive increase in Personal Leadership Velocity when compared to the Lazy Leaders score of 2.4 for the same results.

You can change the numbers in stories to see the impact in your Personal Leadership Velocity. As a Lazy Leader, your goal is to always be more than 1.0. The more you grow your skills, the higher your number will go.

Now let's talk about supporting you as you become a Lazy Leader…

Chapter Five

Adopting the Way of the Lazy Leader

You've read the book so far. You are ready to embrace the Lazy Leader, be the party and maximize your personal leadership velocity.

Now what?

Once you've truly committed in your heart to embrace the Lazy Leader, it's time to take action.

If you're totally new to leadership, use this book to guide you in your approach.

If you've been a leader for a while and are transforming your leadership style, you may experience some of the following.

Six Common Transformation Experiences

1. You may flip flop between styles in the beginning.

If you've been martyr leader for a while, you are going to have to unlearn some behaviors – especially the belief, "It's easier if I do it myself."

Old habits can take time to release.

You may find yourself embracing the Lazy Leader and then committing to do work others in the room could do instead of you.

If this happens, simply:

- Pause.

- Breathe.

- And convert the situation.

Say something like, "You know, as I think about this, I'm wondering if someone else might enjoy taking this on or working with me."

You can do this on the spot, at the end of the meeting or even the next day by picking up the phone and inviting others to play.

If you end up doing the work, don't beat yourself up.

Learn from the experience. At least you are aware someone else should be doing the work. This may be a totally new concept for you!

If you find you are still taking on work regularly, you may want to find a buddy to help you.

Here's how one leader used his buddy...

A leader who just could not let go of doing it all, asked a friend to give him a signal at the meeting if he was taking on work others could do.

The friend would pull her ear. It was subtle so others might not notice – but he did.

The leader was amazed at how many times his friend's ear got pulled at the first meeting.

- He hadn't realized how little he let others participate.

- He thought he was just doing the best for the chapter.

They continued with the ear-pulling cue for a few months.

- The leader got better every meeting.

- It became a game to have a no-ear-pulled meeting.

The leader noticed his volunteers were more engaged than usual and he was less stressed.

The Lazy Leader way was working for him!

Transitioning to a Lazy Leader is going to be two steps forward and one back until you rebuild your habits and develop your skills.

As long as you move in the right direction – celebrate!

In time, being a Lazy Leader will be as natural as breathing.

2. You may grieve at no longer being a martyr.

Let's face it. You may have been a martyr leader for years. It's been a big part of your identity.

- You've worked your fingers to the bone.

- You've had time complaining in front of the chapter and people consoled you.

- You've been so busy for the chapter the dog didn't know who you were.

Your martyr approach made you feel important.

And now it's time to let go.

As a Lazy Leader with a team doing the work, you may find yourself less stressed - and enjoying the success of others.

- It's going to feel sort of foreign for a while.

- You may miss the intense busyness you once knew.

And it's going to be okay.

This is just a transition. Like when you graduated from school to stepped into the real world.

- You may miss some of your martyr days.

- You may fondly remember them.

And know as a Lazy Leader, you are helping to take your chapter to the next level.

If you are truly committed to your chapter's mission, you need to have more people happily engaged with your chapter – and this is the way to do it.

3. People may resist your change at first.

If you've been the go-to, do-it-all person for years, people may be confused as you start to transition to being a Lazy Leader.

You just need to educate them about what's going on with you.

- You are focusing on bringing new people into the chapter.

- You want to create some open time in your life.

- You are working on your leadership skills to ensure the future of the chapter.

If they really don't get it and serve as a leader with you, give them a copy of this book. Let me do the heavy lifting for you.

As you start to give referrals and using a more open process in getting the work done, others may be surprised.

They'll get over it.

They may try to seduce you into your old martyr ways by asking you several times to take on extra work others can do.

They aren't being evil.

- They might think you are over this new kick.

- They may have simply forgotten – remember they've got a long habit of turning to you for everything.

- They might not know how to ask anyone else - a training moment for you.

With time and your continued commitment to being a Lazy Leader, they too will change their habits and start to invite others to get involved.

4. You may feel uncomfortable asking others to help you.

You are used to doing it all. Perhaps previously you thought asking for help made you look weak. Maybe you didn't know how to ask others.

The funny feeling in transition should be fleeting – especially if you truly embrace the Lazy Leader approach.

You are not asking others to help because you are blowing off the work.

- Your job as a leader is to secure the future of your chapter by moving the chapter's mission forward.

- 95% of the time, you can get others involved.

Get over the squeamishness - you're doing the right thing by asking others to help.

5. You feel like you won't have any power if you're not a martyr.

The power of a martyr leader is rather artificial.

Sure, you get to make all the decisions, do all the work - and complain loudly every step of the way – but who is on your team?

Power is about the number of people who you can influence – not how much work you personally do.

As a Lazy Leader, you build your power base with every person you invite to your party – whether a 10% or 40% volunteer.

People will be more likely to look out for you when they feel appreciated and are given the opportunity to make a relevant, meaningful impact while working for you.

In the beginning, especially as you invite others into the decision making process, you may feel like you've lost some sense of control – and you have.

But in exchange, you will be building your volunteer base – and be able to geometrically increase your ability to move your mission forward.

Now that's real power.

6. You worry you aren't doing enough.

There is an interesting side effect of transforming to being a Lazy Leader. You may find yourself more stressed out because you are less stressed in volunteering and have some extra time.

Get used to the relief – it will eventually feel good.

Everything running smoothly, thanks to the help of others, is a sign you are on the right path.

Consider the following story...

Josie committed to being a Lazy Leader just before taking on the chapter's big fundraising project.

At a fabulous kick-off meeting, after everyone helped define what a successful event would look like, Josie helped volunteers divide into teams with specific areas of responsibility.

Every team had a leader and Josie spent time coaching them in getting a solid lift-off for their own teams.

Josie and the leaders chatted regularly and used some online space to share across teams what was going on - and where they could use help.

Two months prior to the event, everything was on schedule and looking very profitable.

Calvin, the past project chair, had been watching Josie very carefully. She didn't look stressed enough. He knew by this point she should be in pure panic - and stay there until the actual event.

Calvin began calling members of Josie's team to see what was going on.

He talked to a few volunteers who didn't know anything about sponsorships! He was mortified. Without sponsorships the project was sunk.

Calvin made a beeline for the chapter president.

"Josie needs to be removed as chair immediately!"

When the president approached Josie, she was just back from a spa appointment. "Don't you think you are being irresponsible going to the spa only a few weeks from the big event? That type of thing should happen AFTER the event. Not before."

Josie was flabbergasted. What was going on?

The president explained Calvin was worried because she wasn't doing enough for the project.

It was a turning point for Josie.

She could have questioned her Lazy Leader approach, jumped in with both feet and taken work away from others so she would appear appropriately busy.

But, Josie was enjoying the experience of leading a fabulous project without breaking a major sweat yet.

She educated the chapter president about her new approach. It seems Calvin spoke to a few 10-20% volunteers who were focused on just their piece of the world – not the entire big project and thus knew nothing about sponsorships.

By the end of the conversation, the president was very impressed with Josie and promised to take care of Calvin.

Josie and her team ran a lovely fundraising event which brought in a **50% increase** of profits over the previous year.

As you embrace the Lazy Leader approach, lean into the experience of less stress. It's good for your heart – and for your chapter.

Three Strategies to Make Your Transformation Smoother

1. Build a support team.

You are about to embark on a new adventure. Invite some friends to join you.

- You won't have to do this alone.

- You can learn from each other.

- It will be more fun.

Here's how one leader did it...

Tina agreed to step up as president - even though the chapter was struggling to stay afloat.

Just a few years ago, the chapter won many awards. Only a few die-hards were left.

Tina was not one of them.

She had belonged for a few years, showed up fairly regularly - but had no interest in the martyr style of leadership which dominated the chapter.

To her surprise, one day Ralph who was currently President for the second time, asked her to grab coffee with him.

The outcome of the conversation?

The current board wanted her to step up to leadership. They were tired and thought she could bring new life to the chapter.

Tina told Ralph she had no interest in being consumed by the chapter - with her young family at home it was impossible.

Ralph assured her the board knew about her children and willing to support her as they could.

Tina cautioned. "If I do this, I'm not going to be a martyr leader. I'm going to get others involved."

Tina was worried about the older leaders putting on pressure to adopt their ways once she got started.

She decided to create a support team to help her be a successful president and turn the chapter around.

When she attended the national president-elect training, she clicked with a few leaders from other chapters who also did not want to be martyrs.

They made a pact to check in once a month to serve as sounding boards for each other - and make sure they weren't being consumed by their chapters.

Tina wanted some local support as well.

She bought Lazy Leader books for her entire board.

- As a team they committed to turning
  the chapter around - without ruining their lives.

- Each board meeting, they discussed
  a different chapter from the Lazy Leader book.

- They created challenges and competitions to
  reinforce what they learned from the book.

**Tina wanted to make sure the chapter turned around -
and future leaders were trained to keep it going.**

By the end of Tina's term, the chapter had a new energy to it.

More people were involved.

**They were moving the chapter's mission forward -
and there was a great sense of hope in the air
for continued success.**

Tina's support team of other presidents and her
now well-trained board helped her to lead her chapter
to better health - wihout becoming a marty leader.

**A mentor may also be a great addition to your
support team.**

- You can learn from their mistakes.

- Tap into their experience.

If you don't have friends ready to step up to becoming Lazy Leaders or don't know potential mentors, check out the Chapter Leaders Playground.

Members include volunteer leaders from across organizations who are embracing the Lazy Leader approach and are working on their skills there.

2. Remember to breathe.

There will be moments when old ways rise up and you wonder what you are doing.

The little person in your head will try to cast doubt on the Lazy Leader ways.

When the questioning starts, remember to breathe.

- Breathing helps to release the stress and keeps your mind engaged.

- Tell the little person "Not useful" until they get the hint and go away.

- (When they do, you'll feel the release in your body and feel calmer in your commitment.)

Know you are on the right path. You are making a difference. You are moving your chapter's mission forward better than you ever have before.

Just remember to breathe.

3. Celebrate your successes.

Catch yourself making new decisions or inviting others to join your party.

- Appreciate the effort you are making.

- Reward yourself for not taking on work others could do.

- Keep a journal or notes to document how far you've come and review your progress regularly.

When you adopt the way of the Lazy Leader, you start on a new and exciting learning adventure.

Make it a fun one.

Now let's explore five basic skill sets to help your transformation...

Chapter Six

Five Basic Skill Sets
Lazy Leaders Master

As you transition into the Lazy Leader approach to achieve outrageous results, you'll be using some new skills to support your success.

Here are some strategies to help you in the process.

Become a Master of Referrals

Many volunteer leaders worry if they say "no" when asked to help they will:

- Hurt feelings.

- Miss an important opportunity.

- Wreck their reputation.

In reality, most leaders ask busy people to help out – because they will say "yes" and find a way to get it done.

Probably 85% of the time, you are asked to help out on something with little to do with your special skills and talents. They just wanted the work done and felt they could trust you to do it.

- "We need someone to make 50 phone calls in the next two days and thought you would be brilliant."

- "We really need you to pick up this other project too."

- "Can you arrive at the meeting early to make sure this happens?"

All of these requests will soak up your time – and could be done by others.

In other words, you need to become a master at referring others to help out.

Giving a great referral can be more valuable than doing the work yourself.

- You involved another person in moving your chapter's mission forward.

- They may have skill, talent and/or passion for the action requested.

- You increase your Personal Leadership Velocity.

The basic referral has a sweet-sour-sweet approach:

- Thank you for asking. (sweet)

- I need to turn you down. (sour)

- Olivia would be a fabulous fit. Why don't you ask her? (sweet)

You may add some details to the above wording – like explain why Olivia would be fabulous to sell them on the additional value of asking her.

Be interested in meeting new people and learning what they want from volunteering.

In order to be a master referrer you need to know people to refer to others. A real pro will also be aware of the special gifts, talents and interests of others.

Encourage those who you give a referral to make sure they mention you provided their name.

It lets people know you are looking out for them.

You may want to do a quick check in with your referral at the next chapter meeting or via email to see how it's going for them. Are they enjoying the work?

The follow up contact continues to build your relationship with them - and strengthens your position as the Lazy Leader in the know.

Become a Master at Including Members

Part of being the party is inviting others to play with you. It also means when they show up at an event or meeting, there is something meaningful for them to do.

Here are five ways you can include others:

1. In defining the big picture of your project.

Volunteers are more enthusiastic if they help create the vision of success.

2. Brainstorming solutions to chapter challenges.

Sometimes the leadership team can get in a rut with their thinking. Inviting others to the discussion opens the doors for fresh ideas.

Here's how one chapter energized their members...

A chapter with 500 members had only a handful active in the chapter. The board had worked for years to turn this ship – with little success.

They decided to host a "Brainstorming at the Bar" event to discuss how to make the chapter more valuable to members.

We created a fun invitation and emailed it to all members – three times. Two weeks out, one week out plus the day before the party.

Board members also made a few personal calls.

About 30 people showed up for the brainstorming – almost twice the number of people who normally showed for meetings!

The message they delivered was loud and clear. There were people in the chapter who still cared - but didn't find value in the meetings.

The group continued to meet at the bar and grew every month.

Many of them still don't attend chapter meetings –
but now find ways to move the mission forward and
feel more connected to their chapter.

The leaders implemented some of the suggestions from
the brainstorming and chapter meeting attendance has
grown as well.

3. Throw a party to get busy work done.

It doesn't take magical skills to stuff envelopes,
fold newsletters or prepare name badges for a big event.

If your team has a bunch of busy work tasks needed
to be done – why suffer alone?

Throw a party and invite the rest of the chapter to help out.

As a fun, two-hour commitment you may find new people
willing to help out.

If no one new shows, there are still benefits. The word is out
about your team being fun – and your team members will
enjoy the party energy as they get the work done.

4. Promote pickup volunteer work to members.

Any Saturday at the gym, you'll find people playing a game
of pickup basketball. There's no formal league involved.
They don't promise to show up every week. Whoever is
supposed to be there, shows that day.

How can you create and promote pickup volunteer opportunities in your chapter?

- The opportunities should be relevant, meaningful – and appreciated.

- They should also require no long-term commitment.

Committees can play a role in pickup volunteer work.

- Do committees periodically host work parties as describe above?

- Do you need a surge of volunteers for just an hour or two at an event?

- Do committees invite members to join in various discussions to deepen the diversity around the table?

5. Use your website to support a 15-Minute Club.

- Create a list of ways members can help the chapter when they have an extra 15 minutes.

- Explain how to report their effort so you know they helped.

- Share the results and impact: How many people? How many hours logged?

- Celebrate together: Could be virtually or maybe a quarterly party to keep volunteers connected – even if they don't tend to show up to anything else in person.

There is an endless number of ways you can tap into the wealth of skills, knowledge and talent your members bring to the table.

Become a Master of Tapping into Other Resources

Your members are only one slice of the resources you'll want to tap into as a Lazy Leader. There are many others who can also help you get more done with less effort.

1. Other organizations similar to yours.

There may be local chapters of similar organizations who complement your mission. They can be a great source for:

- Cross-promoting regular events.

- Sharing costs of speakers – especially those from out of town.

- Swapping trainers or board retreat facilitators.

- Collaborating on mega-events.

- Creating a great networking event.

Here's how one chapter made it happen...

Donald's chapter participated in regional activities for his association.

Donald loved hearing what other chapters were doing – and wished the other chapters were closer so they could work together on different things.

Donald talked his board into creating a similar type of group locally. It was going to be a networking group for leaders who ran chapters focused on similar missions.

Donald sent out invitations to the first meeting - and followed up with personal calls to boost attendance.

Since this was a get to know each other meeting, the agenda focused on helping attendees get to know each other - and to make connections.

After a warm welcome from Donald and quick round of personal introductions, they took turns answering the following questions:

- What does your organization do?

- What's coming up?

- What kind of help could you use?

Potential solutions were offered on the spot.

Almost everyone walked away with two or three new resources to help their own chapters.

They decided to meet twice a year – and stay in touch electronically until then.

Donald was thrilled with the new network!

2. Your local chamber of commerce.

Your local chamber can bring a bevy of resources
to your chapter and team.

You might use them to:

- Acquire speakers for chapter meetings.

- Tap specialists to give you some feedback.

- Find needed talent and leadership to join your team.

Many chamber members are small business owners who
may enjoy helping you out as a way to increase exposure
for their businesses.

3. Your local community colleges.

Also offer diverse possibilities for you to tap in to.

- Affordable meeting space.

- Expertise in various areas.

- Students who might be willing to help your team
as part of a project for a class.

4. Online relationships.

You and/or your team members may have online connections
willing to give advice.

People don't have to be physically present to provide answers to a challenge or open doors.

Your answers may be simply an email away.

Check out social networking sites such as:

- LinkedIn

- Facebook

- Chapter Leaders Playground

As a Lazy Leader who wants to achieve outrageous results, you must be constantly looking for potential resources you can tap into so you and your team get more done with less effort.

Become a Master
at Developing Others

As a Lazy Leader, you may need to help develop the decision making and leadership skills of others on your team.

For years, you've given them all the answers. Now you need your team members to start doing more of the thinking.

They may resist at first.

Build their confidence by coaching them through the process - pull the answers from them.

Imagine the following...

Josh has committed to being a Lazy Leader. Susan, a volunteer on his team, asks Josh what is the best way to promote the big event.

In the past, Josh would have given her a list of action steps and people to contact.

This time, Josh asks Susan, "You've worked on a few of these events. What do you think?"

Susan stammers, "Huh? What do I think? Who cares? What do you want me to do?"

Josh, with his new Lazy Leader ears can hear how much he squelched Susan in the past by her comments. "Susan, seriously, what do you think would be the three best actions your team can take to promote the event?"

(Josh is now working on pulling the information from Susan. By narrowing the request to three actions, he is giving her some focus.)

Susan doesn't quite believe what she's hearing - and expects Martyr Josh to start spouting orders.

It doesn't happen.

Susan tentatively offers a few suggestions.

Josh acknowledges her ideas and asks her for more information, "Those are some good ideas Susan. How do you think your team could get them started?"

The conversation continues back and forth. Josh keeps asking Susan questions to help her flush out her plan.

Susan brings up a new form of promotion. Old Josh would have rejected it vehemently, "That's not how we do things!"

Lazy Leader Josh keeps an open mind and talks to Susan about how she will measure the effectiveness of all her ideas.

At the end of the meeting, Susan hops in her car and calls her best friend in the chapter, "You will NEVER believe what just happened! Josh made me come up with the promotion plan - and even bought our new idea!

"Then he asked some great questions. Most I knew the answers too – but a few I didn't. Did you ever think he'd let us do this? I'm so excited. I hope he doesn't change his mind."

By taking the time to pull good decisions and plans from your volunteers, you help to maximize your Personal Leadership Velocity. You are also training the future leaders of your chapter.

It's another Lazy Leader win-win.

Become a Master at Honing Your Own Leadership Skills

As you have probably figured out, the Lazy Leader who gets outrageous results is actually a very skilled leader.

Rather than focus on doing all the work, they work on polishing the skills which support them in attracting more people on their team and working with them effectively.

Some of the skills you'll want to polish include:

- Delegating

- Communicating

- Problem solving

- Networking

- And more.

To help you in your quest, I've included a list of resources designed specifically for chapter leaders at the end of this book.

Now some FAQs and coaching from me...

Chapter Seven

Frequently Asked Questions

Q: Cynthia, isn't "lazy" a bad word?

A: Usually lazy is simply another's perception.

For example, if others don't see you panicked, stressed out and near burnout as a chapter leader, they may call you lazy.

In reality, if you use the strategies we've talked about in this book, you will be easily accomplishing all they do in less time with less effort.

To me, that's being effective and smart – not lazy in a bad way.

Q: Why did you use the term "Lazy Leader" in this book?

A: Think about it. If I named the book, The Efficient Leader, how much fun would that be?

It wouldn't get half the word of mouth promotion the Lazy Leader generates.

Plus, I've worked with volunteer leaders for more than ten years.

I've seen leaders try a more efficient route and been beat up by others for "not doing it right" – and being lazy.

My hope is by taking on the perception of the Lazy Leader, we can grow our chapters and move our missions forward more easily.

The world needs us!

Q: Why do you capitalize "Lazy Leader" throughout the book?

I want you to remember to think about being a Lazy Leader with new eyes.

Being a Lazy Leader is a wonderful gift to give others and society.

Q: I notice you use martyr leader as a contrast to Lazy Leader. Don't you think that's a bit extreme?

I did it for two reasons.

First I want to make sure you see the contrast in approaches.

Second, I also believe many leaders do not realize what they have become and the effect on the chapter.

Many current leaders started out as strong worker bees for the chapter.

They were promoted to leadership because they got work done – not because they were wonderful at inviting others to get involved.

The worker bee promotion has become institutionalized in too many chapters.

Leaders get the work done and grumble all the way.

They have forgotten or never learned the people skills, management skills and leadership approaches needed to get others involved.

The do-it-all martyrs are tired and burning out.

The future of many chapters is at risk.

I needed to drive home the point in very clear language – and hopefully open some eyes to another way.

Q: I don't appreciate being called a martyr. I worked hard for my chapter for years.

I know. It's time to let others help carry the load.

Using the term martyr is not meant as an insult to anyone – it's just an observation.

If I hit a nerve, maybe it's time for you to consider embracing the Lazy Leader approach.

Q: Are you encouraging the quality of work to go down? You told us to embrace the Lazy Leader within.

How will we keep our standards?

A: I never promoted dropping quality.

Embracing the Lazy Leader is about building a team who will work together to achieve goals.

You may find as you hone your skills in working with your team, the quality of work and its impact actually goes up!

Q: What's the deal with 10% vs. 110% volunteers? I was always taught to give it my all because I'll only get out of the chapter what I put into it.

A: If you look back, the 100% volunteer and expectation for extreme commitment or loyalty started decades ago – when there weren't a lot of options for how people spent their time. The Internet didn't exist - nor did TV. Mom stayed home and made everything from scratch including bread and butter.

Over the years, the 100% volunteer became rather institutionalized.

Only people who throw their life out of balance for the good of the chapter are worthy of being leaders or valued by the chapter.

Reality is we live in a different world than when those norms were originally created.

There are wonderful people who want to be involved but may only be able to volunteer at a 10 % or 20% level.

That needs to be okay and celebrated too.

I've heard stories from older volunteers who were given time off work when they became president of their local chapter and a year of leave if they stepped up to a national board.

Today, such extreme company support sounds more like an urban myth!

As such, our chapters need to embrace the Lazy Leader approach. Making it okay for a 50% volunteer to lead a team of people who will get the work done – but not necessarily break into the same sweat as one person doing all the work.

Embracing volunteers who commit less than 100% is key to the future of your chapter.

Q: I like doing a lot of volunteer work – and am proud of what I've done.

Am I now supposed to throw it all away? Those organizations will hurt if I'm not there to do the work!

A: This book focuses on the volunteer leader – not the hands-on volunteers.

If you enjoy doing volunteer outreach, then do it.

People like you play an important role in our society.

On the other hand, if you are a chapter officer or committee chair, your job is to move the mission forward by doing a slice of chapter work – through volunteer efforts of others.

Too many people have accepted a leadership position and then do all the work – rather than involve others.

If you are a volunteer leader, then yes, I would encourage you to learn some new skills and try out the Lazy Leader way.

You'll strengthen the team of people supporting your organization – and be able to make a bigger impact too.

A real win-win.

Q: The Lazy Leader concept is nice. But let's get real. People don't want to get involved and volunteer. They never do what they promise to do on my committees – and rarely even come back to a meeting!

A: Hmmm… the latest research, including the American Society of Association Executives Decision to Volunteer study (2008) of 26,305 members and non-members, found people are volunteering - and want to make a meaningful impact.

• The challenge is they want a different experience than what used to work in the volunteer world.

• They want to be part of the action – not simply worker bees.

If your volunteers show up once and don't come back it may be your approach needs to be adjusted to work with these new demands.

My <u>Go Team Go! Leading Today's Teams to Victory</u>
book will walk you through step-by-step how to launch a
committee/board and keep them happily committed.

It would be a great place for you to start.

**Q: Won't people think I'm a bad person if
I turn them down when they ask me for
help? I've always said "yes" in the past.**

A: Having boundaries is not about being a bad person.

**Probably 85% of the time, you are asked to do something
because people know you will do it – not because of
some special gift or talent you have.**

Therefore, if you turn the busy work down with a referral
to someone else who might do the work, you are still helping
to get the work done – which helps them achieve their goal.

Specific steps about how to gracefully make the referral
can be found in chapter six.

**Q: I've been doing all the work for years.
New members don't want to volunteer and
quite frankly it makes me mad!**

**You must be kidding yourself to think this
Lazy Leader approach will work.**

**Cynthia, I see it as a recipe for disaster.
What are you thinking?**

A: I can hear your anger and frustration and am sorry for your experience.

It sounds like you've been working very hard on behalf of your chapter for quite a while.

It also sounds like you would appreciate some relief – as long as the work gets done properly.

I'm going to guess you are looking for others like you – volunteers who give 110% from the get go.

When new volunteers fail to show up for a second meeting you've been disappointed – and even more frustrated.

If you could find a way to celebrate a team of people who may individually only do say, 10-25% of their potential; however, as a team make up the full job, you will find the support you want sooner and with more ease.

I'm even wondering if you've done so much for so long, your skills for inviting others to be involved at say a 10% level to your 110% commitment are a tad rusty?

My advice would be to really commit to the Lazy Leader approach and then work on your skills in attracting the volunteers who want to do some but not all of the work.

We run programs all the time on the Chapter Leaders Playground around this issue.

Checking them out would be a great way for you to learn these skills - and build a personal support team of others embracing the Lazy Leader way.

Q: I was appointed committee chair because I was one of the hardest workers on the team last year.

If I suddenly shift to a Lazy Leader way, I will be doing a bait and switch to those who trusted me to get the work done.

Wouldn't that make me unethical?

A: I'm not sure where the ethical violation comes in.

If you were appointed chair because the board can trust you to get the work done based on your past performance, using a Lazy Leader approach lets no one down.

Sure you may not be hassling as much as last year or frantic with stress – but you will have a team of volunteers happily working on behalf of the chapter to get the promised work done.

Let's think about your impact….

You not only got the work done, you also were the leader who helped involve more members.

Those happily involved members are more likely to renew their dues – and perhaps become leaders like you in the future too.

Sounds like a winner to me!

Q: I like the concept of the Lazy Leader; however worry about trusting others to get work done – especially when work and life can change on a dime these days.

A: Being a Lazy Leader means embracing the concept that you will have many volunteers who may only give 10-25% effort.

It's normal that life may periodically take a priority over volunteering - so plan to be prepared for it.

- When you launch your team, agree as a group what specific steps to take when life gets in the way.

- Break big tasks into smaller check points to prevent your team from getting massively behind on anything.

- Celebrate your team's forward movement at every meeting so everyone is aware of where others are - and can offer to help if needed.

You can also build some extra cushion into your timeline with your milestones.

If you want more specifics, check out my <u>Go Team Go! Leading Today's Teams to Victory</u> book. It spells out the details of this supportive approach.

Q: I took your Lazy Leader advice - and it totally bombed. I told people what they needed to do. I left them alone. And come deadline time, we had major gaps in our work.

It was one big mess! No more Lazy Leader for me!

Congratulations on being willing to try out the Lazy Leader way. You got the main idea of involving others.

Sounds like you may need some fine-tuning on managing a team of working volunteers.

While you need to invite and allow others to be involved, there also needs to be some system or process for making sure the team is moving forward as needed.

When you build in regular reports and mini-milestones in your process, you won't have a last minute crisis any more.

Q: I like the power I get from being a 110% volunteer leader. I don't want to give the power up.

Your Lazy Leader approach sounds like it will turn me into nothing in my chapter!

A: I understand enjoying power and feeling important.

Working yourself to the bone for the good of the chapter is just one way to do it.

Being a Lazy Leader is a different approach to working with power.

Instead of just getting the project done, as a Lazy Leader
you build a team of volunteers more committed to the chapter
– who also think the world of you.

Think about it...

When you invite others to find ways to make a meaningful
impact in a ways relevant to them, you give them a gift.

**Your power base grows because your influence
has expanded way beyond just getting a project done.**

If anything, the Lazy Leader approach is a way to take you
to the next level of power.

Q: You encourage using technology to support managing teams of volunteers, but I don't know how to use online workspace. What should I do?

A: Online workspace can be wonderful time saver and
enthusiasm generator when used well.

If you don't know how to use it, there are probably others
who don't as well.

Why not hold a training program for those new to it?

Any time you think a new skill, process or product
might help you be more effective as a leader –
but aren't familiar with how to use or do it, providing
training is a great next step.

- There may be folks in your chapter who can serve as trainers.

- And others who would like to learn too.

Offering leadership training and skill development can support the growth of your chapter's Lazy Leaders – and be a neat benefit of membership too.

Q: What kinds of decisions can volunteers make for a project?

It depends.

- Let's assume we are talking about volunteers who are not on your board.

- They are the volunteers who will be helping you out with a project or your area of responsibility.

At your kick-off meeting, you will share the "must have" elements and create as a group the definition of success.

As a team, you can involve volunteers in almost any decision.

If you set up committees on your project, they will be making decisions relevant to their assignment.

(Make sure you provide any must-haves for their work.)

Train the folks who will be serving as chairs on spending and budget issues.

- What kind of communication do you need from them?

- Do you want them to create a team plan before spending money or taking major directional action?

- Can they make decisions as long as they are within their budget?

- At what point do they need to talk to you?

- Who signs contracts in your chapter?

The more clear you are with yourself about what is truly a must have and what is a preference, the easier it becomes to encourage volunteer decisions.

Preferences are just that – preferences. Space for others to leave their thumbprints.

Q: I tried your Lazy Leader approach at my chapter meeting last night.

When people asked me to do work others could do, I gave them a referral. After the second referral, I had people asking me if I was sick. Not sure this is going to work.

A: Congratulations to you for embracing your Lazy Leader and starting to give referrals!

As far as your friends in the chapter go, they were probably just confused by the new you.

They will get used to getting amazing referrals from you –
and may even ask you to coach them on how to be
a Lazy Leader too!

Q: I LOVE the Lazy Leader concept and want to embrace it – but we only have a handful of folks left active in our chapter.

If I become lazy who will do all the work?

A: Way to go on embracing your Lazy Leader!

Now it's time to find those volunteers.

My bet is your chapter has been run by martyrs for quite
a while now.

You may find it easier to transform if you get the rest
of the leaders still involved also committed to becoming
Lazy Leaders.

It will shift the energy of your chapter.

**If they aren't ready to step up, don't despair. You can
change your piece of the chapter world.**

Before you jump into recruiting new members and
volunteers, you need to get clear on what they will be doing.

How will opportunities to help be different than they
were before?

Do you have options for:

- One-time, two-hour commitments?

- Volunteering at midnight?

- Periodic volunteering?

- Committee members at 20% level – rather than 110% volunteers?

Once you get clear on the new options for being involved, you are ready to invite others to your party.

People you might invite include:

- Current members who don't show up much.

- Temporary volunteers.

- Former members still in the area.

- Members who just transferred to your town.

- New graduates who haven't joined yet.

You can invite in person, on the phone or with an invitation to a kick-off party.

You are limited only by your imagination.

If you want detailed steps for a recruiting event, check out my How to Recruit Generation Me book.

It will walk you through hosting a successful event.

Need more affirmation?

Research has found several times the number one reason why people don't get involved is no one asked them.

There are tons of people waiting to be invited to be part of cool experience which supports them in making a meaningful impact – while they are having fun too.

You're going to invest some time on the front end with your recruitment efforts to invite people to get involved.

The payoff will be huge in the shared work and impact you will now be able to make in moving your chapter's mission forward!

Now some final thoughts to help you get started as a Lazy Leader...

Chapter Eight

Final Thoughts

Congratulations on making it to the end of this book.

I hope you now understand the power you'll have and gift you'll give by being a Lazy Leader.

I also hope you are ready to embrace your Lazy Leader within, be the party and maximize your Personal Leadership Velocity as you achieve at outrageous results for your chapter.

The information explored in this book is just the beginning.

As you dig into your transformation, you'll learn more about what works specifically for you.

- I've included a list of resources to help you succeed in your transformation.

- There's also detailed index at the end of this book.

- I want you to be able to easily find information when you beginning to wonder about next steps.

I was serious when I said I want to hear about your transformation and achievements as a Lazy Leader.

Please send me your updates at:
damour@peoplepowerunlimited.com

I know you are going to have some outrageous results to share as you lean into becoming a Lazy Leader.

Here's to your future success as a Lazy Leader!

- Cynthia

Cynthia D'Amour, MBA
Ann Arbor, Michigan

The Lazy Leader's Resource List

The Chapter Leaders Playground

The Chapter Leaders Playground, founded by Cynthia D'Amour is 2007, is an online community for volunteer leaders from across organizations.

At the Playground, you'll discover more than 40 Webinar Playdates each year featuring how-to information you can use right away.

In the Playground Library you'll find dozens of articles by Cynthia spelling out strategies to help you achieve more with less effort.

You'll also find the Lazy Leader's Lounge – which includes an up to date list of resources you can use to be more effective as a Lazy Leader.

http://www.chapterleadersplayground.org

Cynthia D'Amour's Blog

Cynthia blogs on leadership and life. Her blog is a fun, quick read and has been called both quirky and hypnotizing. Every post ends with a question for chapter leaders to think about.

Check it out at: http://cynthiadamour.com

Cynthia D'Amour's Active Member Minute e-mail

Cynthia has been sharing best practices, research findings, and shocking stories with volunteer leaders since 1998. The goal of each issue is to help you get more members involved.

Sign up at the Chapter Leaders Playground at:
http://www.chapterleadersplayground.org

Chapter Leader Books
by Cynthia D'Amour

How to Turn Generation Me into Active Members of Your Association

Cynthia's how-to classic for getting more members involved in your chapter. You'll learn hundreds of strategies for making your chapter the place to be. It's the basic book every chapter leader should have.

How to Recruit Generation Me

Cynthia walks you through how to today's members who expect a meaningful and relevant experience in your chapter. You'll also learn how to run a successful recruiting event.

Members Tell All!

Cynthia collected some of her favorite stories from her Active Member Minute e-zines and converted them into a dynamic leadership training tool you can use with your board and future leaders.

Each story is followed by questions you can use to launch strategic conversations about today's volunteers.

Go Team Go! Strategies for Leading Today's Teams to Victory

Cynthia will teach you the steps of launching a dynamic team filled with today's volunteers. You'll learn how to run committee meetings your members will love to attend.

You'll also learn how to manage diverse teams and get beyond challenges such as "we always do it that way."

Networking: The Skills the Schools Forgot to Teach

As a chapter leader, you need to be confident working the room at chapter events. Cynthia spells out basic skills such as how to start a conversation and keep it going, how to meet multiple people at one event and how to boost your confidence throughout the process.

Are You ONE Relationship Away From BIG Money?

Serving as a chapter leader can be a great way for people to grow their business – if they know how to do it the right way. In your face sales is totally wrong. Cynthia will teach you how to turn casual conversations into avid supporters in a simple, relationship-based approach to doing busing.

CDs and More for Chapter Leaders

Cynthia has a constantly growing collection of CDs and other tools designed to help chapter leaders get more members involved in their association.

Cynthia's books, CDs and more are available
at the **Leadership Shop**
on the Chapter Leaders Playground
http://www.chapterleadersplayground.org

Have Cynthia D'Amour speak at your next meeting

Cynthia is a dynamic, high-energy, hands-on speaker who will get your participants on their feet. She'll teach them specific strategies for succeeding as a Lazy Leader and turning "I don't have time" into "I can't wait to volunteer!"

Cynthia is also a strong facilitator for strategic planning and a fun emcee for high-profile events.

Learn more about Cynthia
potentially speaking for you at
the People Power Unlimited website.
http://www.peoplepowerunlimited.com

Meet Author
Cynthia D'Amour

Having served more than 55 total years on volunteer boards and recruited more than 250 members, Cynthia D'Amour knows firsthand the key issues that association leaders face every day in dealing with today's volunteers.

For more than twelve years, Cynthia D'Amour has worked with association leaders and staff to help get more members involved using a relationship-based approach.

Cynthia has a degree in marketing and has done extensive graduate work in super-accelerated learning, communication skills and family dynamics.

Cynthia earned an MBA from the University of Phoenix with an emphasis on leadership and association management.

The joy of relationship building is in Cynthia's genes.

Her mother makes friends out of strangers everywhere she goes and Cynthia's dad has been president of practically every organization he's ever joined.

With that combination in Cynthia's blood, she's fulfilling her destiny working with chapter leaders!

Cynthia uses her experience as an 8th grade teacher and manager at Macy's to create a fun approach to developing leadership skills and facilitating strategic meetings for associations.

Cynthia is the author of several books including
**How to Turn Generation Me into Active Members
of Your Association, How to Recruit Generation Me,
Go Team Go! Strategies for Leading Today's Teams to
Victory** and **Networking: The Skill the Schools Forgot
to Teach**. She also wrote part of the American Society of
Association Executives book, **The Component Relations
Handbook**.

Cynthia produces a bi-monthly e-zine called Cynthia
D'Amour's Active Member Minute and blogs about
leadership and life at http://cynthiadamour.com.

Cynthia is also the proud founder of the Chapter Leaders
Playground – an online community for volunteer leaders
from across organizations.

Cynthia is based in Ann Arbor, Michigan – home to the
University of Michigan.

Cynthia's parents knew it was true love when their proud
Michigan State graduate was willing to marry a Michigan
man – and move to the center of the evil empire! (Which she
now loves.)

Cynthia's husband James keeps her pointed in the right
direction. Raindrop, official mascot of the Chapter Leaders
Playground, has her own Facebook page and is happy
to work for extra doggy treats.

If you would like to contact Cynthia, you can reach her at
damour@peoplepowerunlimited.com

- Index -

Symbols

A

B